What Allah says about those who deny the Criterion!

Allah says: "Most blessed is He Who sent down this Criterion on His servant, to be a warner to all mankind;" [25 Al-Furqaan:1]

The Arabic word tabaraka is very comprehensive, and cannot be understood fully and completely by "most blessed", not even by a sentence. However, its meanings may be grasped by keeping in view that Allah is the most Exalted, the Greatest, and the Sovereignty of the heavens and the earth belongs to Him. He is the most Beneficent, that is why He has bestowed the great blessing of Al-Furqan (the Qur'an), by degrees, on His servant, so that he may warn all mankind.

The Qur'an has been called Al-Furqan because it is the gauge for judging right and wrong, virtue and vice, truth and falsehood. The word nazzala implies revelation of the Qur'an gradually, by degrees.

"... warner to all mankind." To warn all mankind of the evil consequences of their heedlessness and deviation. The warner may be Al-Furqan, or the Holy Prophet (saws) to whom it was revealed. In fact, both were the warners, because, they were both sent for one and the same purpose. The message of the Qur'an and the Prophethood of Muhammad (saws) were not meant for any particular country, but for the whole world. Not for their own time, but for all times to come. This has been stated at several places in the Qur'an, for instance Allah says:

"(Say, O Muhammad): O men! I am Allah's Messenger to you all - of Him to Whom belongs the dominion of the heavens and the earth. There is no god, but Allah. He grants life and deals death. Have faith then in Allah, and in His Messenger, the ummi Prophet who believes in Allah and His words, and follow him so that you may be guided aright." [7 Al-A`raf: 158];

"Ask them: 'Whose testimony is the greatest?' Say: Allah is the witness between you and I, and this Qur'an was revealed to me that I should warn you thereby and also whomsoever it may reach. Do you indeed testify that there are other gods with Allah? Say: I shall never testify to such a thing. Say: Allah is the One God and I am opposed to all that you associate with Him in His divinity." [6 Al An'am: 19];

"(O Prophet), We have not sent you forth but as a herald of good news and a warner for all mankind. But most people do not know." [34 Saba: 28];

"We have sent you forth as nothing but mercy to people of the whole world." [21 Al Anbiya: 107]

The Holy Prophet (saws) himself has stated this clearly in the Hadith. For instance, he said: "I have been sent to all men, the red, and the black. Before me a Prophet was sent only to his own people, but I have been sent to all mankind." (Bukhari, Muslim).

"I have been sent to all mankind, and I am the Last of the Prophets." (Muslim).

Allah says: "He to Whom belongs the Sovereignty of the heavens and the earth. Who has begotten no son. Who has no partner in His Sovereignty. Who created each and every thing, and then ordained its destiny." [25 Al-Furqaan:2]

Another translation may be: "To Him belongs the Kingdom of the heavens and the earth." That means, He alone has an exclusive right to it, and no one else has any right to it, nor any share in it.

"He has neither any relation of direct parenthood to anyone, nor has He taken anyone as a son. Therefore, none else in the universe is entitled to be worshipped. Allah is Unique and there can be no partner. Thus, all those who associate with Him angels, jinns or saints, as His offspring, are ignorant. Likewise, those who believe that someone, is His "son", are also ignorant. They have no true conception of the Greatness of Allah, and consider Him to be weak and needy, like human beings, who require someone to become their inheritor. It is sheer ignorance and folly."

The Arabic word mulk means Sovereignty, Supreme Authority, and Kingship. Thus, the sentence means: "Allah is the Absolute

Ruler of the whole universe and, there is none other who has any right to authority. Therefore, Allah alone is God." Whenever a man takes anything as his lord, he does so under the presumption that his deity has the power to do good, or bring harm, and make, or mar his fortune. Nobody, would like to worship a powerless deity. Now, when it is recognized that none, but Allah, has the real power and authority, in the universe, nobody will bow before anyone other than Him in worship. Nor sing anybody else's hymns of praise. Nor commit, the folly of bowing in worship before anything else except his real God, or recognize any other, as his ruler, because "To Allah belongs the Sovereignty of the heavens and the earth, and to Him alone."

There may be other translations of this also: "He has ordained it in due proportion," or "He has appointed an exact measure for everything." But no translation can convey its real meaning, which is: "Allah has not only created everything in the universe, but also determined its shape, size, potentialities, characteristics, term of existence, limitations, and extent of its development, and all other things concerning it. Allah has created the means and provisions to enable it to function properly in its own separate sphere."

This is one of the most comprehensive verses of the Qur'an with regard to the Doctrine of the Indivisible Oneness of Allah (Tauhid). According to Traditions, the Holy Prophet (saws) himself taught this verse to every child of his family, as soon as it was able to speak, and utter a few words. Thus, this verse is the best means of impressing the Doctrine of the Indivisible Oneness of Allah on our minds, and every Muslim should use it for educating his children as soon as they develop understanding.

Allah says: "Yet the people have set up, besides Him, deities, who do not create anything, but are themselves created. Who can neither harm nor help even themselves. Who have no power over life or death, nor can they raise up the dead." [25 Al-Furqaan:3]

The words are comprehensive, and cover all the false gods whom the polytheists worship. Whether they are angels, jinns, Prophets, saints, the sun, the moon, the stars, trees, rivers, animals etc., which have been created by Allah, or those which have been created by man, as the idols of stone, and wood, etc.

That means, "Allah has sent down Al-Furqan (Qur'an) on His servant. So that, he may invite the people to the Truth, which they have forsaken, due to heedlessness and waywardness, and warn them of the evil consequences of their folly. The Furqan is being revealed gradually so that he may distinguish right from wrong, and the genuine from the counterfeit."

Allah says: "Those who have rejected the Message of the Prophet, say, "This (Al-Furqan) is a forgery, which this man himself has devised, and some others have helped him at it." What a cruel injustice and an impudent lie! They say, "These things are the writings of the ancients, which he has got copied down for himself, and then these are recited to him in the morning and evening." O Muhammad, say to them, "This has been sent down by Him, Who knows the secret of the heavens and the earth." The fact is, that He is very Forgiving and Merciful." [25 Al-Furqaan:4-6]

This is the same objection which the modern orientalists have raised against the Qur'an, but strange as it may seem, no Companion of the Holy Prophet (saws) ever raised such an objection against him. Nobody ever said, that Muhammad (saws), as a boy, had met Buhairah, the monk, and had attained religious knowledge from him. Nor, did anybody claim that he had obtained all that information from the Christian monks, and Jewish rabbis during the trade journeys in his youth. In fact, they knew that he had never traveled alone, but in the caravans, and if they said such a thing, it would be refuted by hundreds of their own people from the city.

Then, one could ask, if he had gained all that knowledge from Buhairah, when he was about 12, and during trade journeys when he was 25, why did he keep it secret from the people till he became 40? Whereas he did not leave his country even for a single day, but lived for years among his own people in the same city. That is why the people of Mecca dared not bring such an impudent, and baseless charge against him. Their objections related to the time when he claimed to be a Prophet of Allah, and not to the time preceding that claim. Their argument was like this: "This man is illiterate and cannot obtain any knowledge through books. He has lived among us for forty years, but we have never heard from him anything that might have shown that he had any acquaintance with what he is preaching.

Therefore, he must have had the help of other people who copied these things from the writings of the ancients, for him. He learned these things from them, and recites them as Divine Revelations. This is a fraud. So much so, that according to some traditions, they named some of his "helpers," who were the people of the Book, and were illiterate and lived in Mecca. For there can be no greater proof of the "fraud" of Prophethood than to specify its source. However, it looks strange that no argument has been put forward to refute this charge, except a mere denial, as if to say, your charge is an impudent lie. You are cruel and unjust to bring such a false charge against Our Messenger.

The Qur'an is the Word of Allah, Who knows all the secrets in the heavens and the earth. Had their charge been based on facts, it would not have been rejected with contempt, for in that case the disbelievers would have demanded a detailed, and clear answer. However, they realized the strength of the arguments, and did not make such a demand. Moreover, the fact that the "weighty" argument failed to produce any doubt in the minds of the new Muslims, was a clear proof that it was a lie. The puzzle is clearly explained, if we keep in view the prevalent circumstances:

(1) The disbelievers of Mecca did not take any decisive steps to prove their charge, although they could, had there been any truth in their charge. For instance, they could have made raids on the houses of the alleged helpers, and on the house of the Holy Prophet (saws) himself and taken hold of the "material," which was being used in this "fraud", and made it public to expose his Prophethood. This was not difficult for them, because they never hesitated to resort to anything to defeat him, including persecution, as they were not bound by any

moral code.

(2) The alleged helpers were not strangers. They lived in Mecca, and everyone knew well how learned they were. The disbelievers knew, that they could never have helped produce a unique and sublime Book, like the Qur'an, which had the highest literary excellence and merit. That is why none of them challenged the answer to the charge. That is why even those people, who did not know them, considered this pointless. Then if the alleged helpers were such geniuses, why did they not claim to be prophets themselves?

(3) Then, all the alleged helpers were freed slaves who were attached to their former masters even after their freedom, according to the customs of Arabia. Therefore, they could not have been willing accomplices of the Holy Prophet (saws), in this fraud, because their former masters could have coerced them to expose it. The only reason for them to help the Holy Prophet (saws), in his claim, could have been some greed, or interest which, under the circumstances, could not even be imagined. Thus, apparently there was no reason why they should have offended those whose protection, and patronage they needed and enjoyed, and become accomplices in the fraud.

(4) Above all, all these alleged helpers embraced Islam. Could it be possible that those persons, who had helped the Holy Prophet (saws) make his fraud successful, could possibly have become his devoted followers? Moreover, if, for the sake of

argument, it was admitted that they helped him, why was not any of them raised to a prominent rank as a reward of his help? Why were Addas, Yasar and Jabr not exalted to the same status as Abu Bakr, Umar and Abu Ubaidah? Another oddity is, that if the "fraud" of prophethood was being carried on with the help of the alleged helpers, how could it remain hidden from the people, who were the Holy Prophet's closest, and most devoted Companions? Thus, the charge was not only silly and false, but it was also below the dignity of the Qur'an, to give any answer to it. The charge has been cited merely to prove that those people had been so blinded by their opposition to the Truth that they could say anything.

"... He is very Forgiving and Merciful" is very meaningful here. It means that Allah is giving respite to the enemies of the Truth, for He is "Forgiving and Merciful." Otherwise, He would have sent down a scourge to annihilate them because of the false charges they were bringing against the Messenger (saws). It also contains a warning, as if to say, O unjust people! If even now you give up your enmity, and stubborness, and accept the Truth, We shall forgive your previous misdeeds.

Allah says: "They say, "What sort of a Messenger is he that he eats food and moves about in the streets? Why has not an angel been sent down to accompany him, and threaten (the disbelievers)? Or why has not at least a treasure been sent down for him, or a garden given to him for (easy) sustenance?" And the wicked people say, "You are following a man bewitched."*sdfootnote17anc Just see what strange arguments they bring forward with regard to you! They have gone so far astray that they cannot charge anything against you. Highly blessed is He, Who, if He wills, could give you much more, and better things than what they propose for you. (Not one but) many gardens, beneath which rivers flow, and big castles." [25 Al-Furqaan:7-10]

That means, he cannot be a Messenger of Allah because he is a human being like us. Had Allah willed to send a Messenger, He would have sent an angel, and, if at all, a human being was to be sent, he should have been a king, or a millionaire, who would have resided in a castle and been guarded by attendants. A Messenger could not be an ordinary person, who has to move about in the marketplaces like the common people, for it is obvious that such a human Messenger cannot attract the attention of the people. In other words, they thought that a Messenger was not meant to guide the people to the right path, but to coerce them to obedience by show of worldly power and grandeur.

That means, "If a human being was to be sent as a Messenger, an angel should have been appointed to accompany him to proclaim: If you do not believe in him, I will punish you." But what son of a Messenger is he, who has to suffer from abuse and persecution?

That is, "If nothing else, Allah should at least have made extraordinary arrangements for his livelihood. However, this man has no treasure and no gardens, yet, he claims to be a Messenger of the Lord of the universe."

The disbelievers of Mecca made false propaganda against the Holy Prophet (saws) that he had been bewitched by some jinn, or by the sorcery of an enemy, or by the curse of some god or goddess, for his insolence. It is strange that they also admitted that he was a clever man, who could make use of extracts from the ancient writings for the sake of his "prophethood", could practice sorcery and was also a poet.

As these objections were frivolous and meaningless, like others, the Qur'an has ignored them, saying, "Your objections are irrelevant, unreasonable and void of sense. You bring no sound argument to prove your doctrine of polytheism, or to refute the Doctrine of the Indivisible Oneness of Allah put forward by him. Whereas, the Messenger (saws) gives such proofs of the Doctrine of the Indivisible Oneness of Allah that you cannot refute them except by saying, He is bewitched. The same is true of the doctrine of life after death, and of the moral system of the Qur'an, which has produced men of high character. You cannot deny these things. You reject them, saying, "He is a human being like us, etc."

Here again the word tabaraka has been used, and in the context it means: "Allah has full control over everything and has unlimited powers. If Allah wills to favor somebody, He can do so as, and when, He wills, without hindrance."

Allah says: "The fact of the matter is that these people have denied "the Hour." And for the one who denies the coming of the Hour, We have prepared a blazing Fire. When it will see them from afar, they will hear the sounds of its raging and roaring. And, when they are chained together and flung into a narrow space therein, they will begin to call for death. (Then it will be said to them:) "Do not call for one death today, but call for many deaths." [25 Al-Furqaan:11-14]

The word As-Sa'at, meaning the Time or the Hour, has been used in the Qur'an as a term for the promised Hour of Resurrection. When all human beings, of all ages will be raised from the dead, and gathered together before Allah Almighty, to account for their beliefs and deeds, right or wrong, and rewarded or punished accordingly.

That means, "The objections they are raising are not due to the reason that they doubt the authenticity of the Qur'an, on some rational ground, or that they do not believe in you for the reason that you eat food, and walk about in the streets like the common people, or that they did not accept your Message of Truth, only because you were not escorted by an angel, or were not given a treasure. The real reason why they are putting forward all sorts of absurd arguments, to reject your Message, is that they do not believe in life after death, and this denial has made them free from all moral obligations. For when one denies life after death, there remains no need for him to consider, and decide what is true or false, or what is right or wrong, etc. Their argument is like this: There is going to be no life after this one, on the earth, when we will be called to account for our deeds before Allah.

Death will be the end of everything, and it will, therefore, make no difference whether one was a worshipper of Allah, a disbeliever, a polytheist, or an atheist, when the ultimate end is to become one with the dust. There is no need for judging what is right, and what is wrong except by the test of success and failure in this life. Those who deny the Hereafter also see that worldly success, or failure does not entirely depend upon one's faith or conduct. Nay, they very often see that the righteous, and the wicked persons, meet with the same end irrespective of their faith, for which there is no ordained punishment or reward in this life.

One righteous person may be living a life of hardship while another enjoying all the good things of life. One wicked person may be suffering for his misdeeds, while the other is enjoying a life of pleasure and plenty. As such, as far as the worldly consequences of adopting a particular moral attitude are concerned, the disbelievers, in the Hereafter, cannot be satisfied whether it is right or wrong. In view of this, those, who deny the Hereafter, do not see any need to consider an invitation to faith and morality, even if it is presented in a most forceful way.

"The Fire will see them" The words used in the Text may be figurative, or they may mean that the Fire of Hell will be endowed with the faculties of seeing, thinking and judging.

Allah says: "Ask them "Is this (Fire) better, or the everlasting Garden, which has been promised to the God-fearing righteous people?" Which will be the recompense of their good deeds, and the final destination of their journey, wherein, they will get everything they desire, and wherein they will dwell forever. This is a promise which your Lord has taken upon Himself to fulfill." [25 Al-Furqaan:15-16]

> Literally: "It is a promise whose fulfillment can be demanded (from Allah)."

Here one may ask the question: How can the promise of the Garden, and the threat of the Fire produce any effect on the attitude of a person who denies Resurrection, and the existence of Paradise and Hell? In order to understand the wisdom, of this method of warning, one should keep in view that it is meant to appeal to the self-interest of a stubborn person, who does not otherwise listen to such arguments. This is, as if to say, "Even if, for the sake of argument, there is no proof of the reality of life after death, there is also no proof that such an event will not occur at all, and there is a possibility for both.

In the latter case, the Believer and the disbeliever both, will be in one and the same position, but if there is life, in the Hereafter, as the Prophet (saws) asserts, then the disbelievers will be doomed to utter ruin". Therefore, such an approach breaks the stubbornness of the disbelievers, and proves to be highly effective when the entire scene of Resurrection, gathering of the people, their accountability, and of Hell and Heaven is presented in a vivid manner, as if the Prophet (saws), had himself, seen it with his own eyes.

Allah says: "And on that Day (your Lord) will gather all these people together as well as their deities, whom they worship besides Allah. Then He will ask them, "Did you mislead these servants of Mine, or did they themselves go astray?" [25 Al-Furqaan:17]

Here, deities do not mean idols, but the angels, the prophets, the saints, the martyrs and the pious men, whom the polytheists, of different communities, have made their deities. Such dialogues between Allah and the gods of the disbelievers occur at several places in the Qur'an. For instance, in Chapter Saba it has been stated: "On the day when He will gather them all together, He will ask the angels, 'Did these people worship you?' They will answer, Glory be to Thee! Thou art our Patron, and not they: They, in fact, worshiped the jinns (that is, satans). Most of these believed in them."

Similarly in Chapter 5 Al-Ma'idah, it is said: "And when Allah will say "O Jesus, son of Mary, did you ever say to the people: Make me and my mother gods instead of Allah? He will answer, Glory be to Thee! It did not behoove me to say that which I had no right to say...I told them only that which Thou didst bid me: Worship Allah, Who is my Lord as well as your Lord."

Allah says: "They will answer, "Glory be to Thee! We dared not take any guardian besides Thee: (they were misled because) Thou didst give them, and their forefathers all the good things of life till they forgot the Warning, and incurred the punishment." Thus will your gods deny all that you are professing today. Then you shall neither be able to repel your punishment, nor shall you get any help from anywhere. Whosoever is guilty of sin among you, We shall make him taste a severe torment." [25 Al-Furqaan:

18-19]

That means, "They were mean people: You gave them all the provisions of life so that they may show gratitude to You, but they became ungrateful, and ignored all the warnings given by the Prophets."

"On that Day your religion, which you now believe, to be true, will prove to be false and even your gods, whom you yourselves have set up, will declare it to be a lie. For none of them ever asked you to make them your deities, and worshipped them as such. Consequently, instead of interceding on your behalf; they will bear witness against you."

"... who will be guilty of sin ...": " .... who will be unjust to the Reality, the Truth and guilty of disbelief and shirk? "The context shows that those who reject the Prophet (saws) and set up other deities instead of Allah and deny life in the Hereafter, are guilty of evil.

Allah says: "O Muhammad, all the Messengers whom We sent before you also ate food, and moved about in the streets. In fact, We have made you all a means of test for one another. Will you show patience, for your Lord sees everything?" [25 Al-Furqaan: 20]

This is an answer to the objection of the disbelievers of Mecca that Muhammad (saws) could not be a Messenger of Allah because he ate food, and moved about in the streets. They have been told that all the Messengers of Allah who came before Muhammad (saws) like Noah, Abraham, Ishmael, Moses and many others whom they knew and acknowledged, as Prophets, and Messengers of Allah also ate food, and walked about in the streets. Nay, even Prophet Jesus, son of Mary, himself, whom the Christians had made the son of Allah (and whose image had also been placed in the Ka`bah by the disbelievers of Mecca) ate food, and walked about in the streets like a common man even according to the Gospels themselves.

It is obvious that the Messenger (saws) and the Believers were a test, for the disbelievers, as to whether, they would believe even after hearing the Divine Message and seeing their pure character. On the other hand, the disbelievers were a test for the Messenger (saws), and his followers in the sense, that they were a means of proving, and trying their true Faith by their persecution. For it is this test alone, which helps to discriminate the true Believers from the hypocrites. That is why, at first, only the poor and the helpless, but sincere people embraced Islam. Had there been no persecution and hardships, but prosperity, wealth and grandeur, the worshippers of the world, and the selfish people would have been the first to embrace Islam.

That means, "Now when you have understood the wisdom of the test, by persecution, it is hoped that you will endure all kinds of hardships without complaint, and willingly undergo the persecutions that are inevitable."

"Your Lord Sees everything." probably means two things:

* First, the way your Lord is conducting your affairs, is according to His will, and nothing that happens is without His knowledge.

* Second: He is fully aware of your sincerity and righteousness in serving His cause under all kinds of hardships. You should therefore rest assured that you will have your full reward. He also sees the persecution and evil of the disbelievers; therefore they will not escape the consequences of their wickedness.

Allah says: "Those people, who have no fear of coming before Us, say, "Why should not the angels be sent down to us? Or else we should see our Lord." Great arrogance have they assumed in regard to themselves, and have violated all limits in their rebellion. The Day, when they will see the angels, will not be a day of rejoicing for the criminals. They will cry out, "May Allah save us!" Then We shall turn to what they have done, and render it vain, like scattered dust. (On the contrary) only those who have deserved the Garden, will have a good abode on that Day, and a cool place for midday rest. On that Day, a cloud will appear tearing the sky, and the angels will be sent down rank after rank. The real Kingdom on that Day will belong only to the Merciful, and it will be a very hard Day for the disbelievers. The unjust man will bite at his hand and say, "Would that I had stood by the Messenger! O, woe to me! Would that I had not chosen so and so for a friend! For it was he, who had deluded me to reject the Warning, which had come to me. Satan has proved a very treacherous man." And the Messenger will say, "O my Lord, my people had made this Qur'an the object of their ridicule." [25 Al-Furqaan:21-30]

That means, "If Allah had really intended to convey His Message to us, He would not have chosen a prophet and sent an angel only to him, but to each one of us individually with the guidance, or He should have sent a deputation of angels to appear before the people with the Message". The same objection has been stated in Chapter Al-An`am thus: "When a Revelation comes before them, they say, `We will not believe in it unless we are given the like of what has been given to the Messengers of Allah.' Allah knows best whom to entrust with His Mission and how it should be enforced."

> That is, Allah Himself should appear before us and make the appeal.

Another translation could be: "They have formed a very high opinion of their own selves."

This very theme has been expressed in much greater detail in [6 Al An'am: 8] "They also say: 'Why has no angel been sent down to this Prophet?' Had We sent down an angel, the matter would surely have long been decided and no respite would have been granted them."

The unbelievers objection is refuted by this remark. It warns them that the time available for accepting the true faith and bringing about the required reform in their lives will last only as long as the Ultimate Reality remains concealed from human perception by the wheel of the Unseen. Once that wheel is removed, there will be no more respite. The summons to Allah's rekoning will have come. This earthly life is a test of whether a man is able to recognize the Ultimate Reality, by the correct exercise of his reason, and intellect. Even though it lies hidden from his sensory perception. In addition, whether, having once recognized it, he is able to behave in conformity with that Reality, by exercising control over his animal self, and its lusts. This test requires that the Reality should remain concealed. Thereafter, man will be confronted with the result of the test rather than by any further test. Until Allah has decided to bring the term of their test to a close, it is not possible to respond to such requests of sending angels to them, in their true form.

(See also note 228 Al-Baqarah) These words are indicative of an important fact. Man's test lies in showing whether he accepts reality, even though he cannot perceive it directly through his senses. And, whether, after having accepted it, he has the moral stamina to obey Allah, even though he is endowed with the capacity to disobey Him. In sending the Prophets, in revealing the Scriptures, indeed, even in performing miracles, Allah has always taken care to leave scope for testing man's power of judgement, and his moral stamina. He has never disclosed reality to such a degree that man would be compelled to accept it. For if that were done, nothing would remain to be tested and the very idea of man's success or failure would be meaningless. It is pointed out, therefore, that people should not keep waiting for Allah and the angels, the devoted servants of His realm, to appear before them.

If that were to happen, it would mark the end of everything, and there would be no occasion left for man to decide anything. To believe, and to bow in submission and obedience to Allah are of value only so long as the reality is presented in such a way as to make its rejection possible. For, if the Truth were to be fully disclosed, and if men were to see with their own eyes Allah on His Throne of Majesty, with the entire universe acting according to His command, what would be the worth of their faith and obedience? If all these things were physically observable, not even the most stubborn unbelievers, and the worst sinners would dare either to disbelieve or disobey. Acceptance of faith and obedience has value only as long as there remains a veil over reality. The moment when reality is totally unveiled, would mark the end of the period granted to man to decide, and of the testing period for him. It would, in fact, be the Day of Judgement.

[15 Al-Hijr:7-8] "Why do you not bring down angels upon us if you are indeed truthful?" We do not send down the angels (in frivolity). When We do send them down, We do so with Truth. Then people are granted no respite.

We do not send down the angels for the mere fun of it, or in response to the request of the people. Nor are they sent, to unveil the reality before them in order to show to them all the unseen things to which the Messengers invite them to believe. As a matter of fact, angels are sent down on that occasion when it is decreed to pass judgment on sane, wicked people. At that time the judgment comes into operation without extending any invitation to the condemned people to accept the message, for their period of respite ends as soon as the reality is unveiled before them. "Except with truth."

They bring down truth with them. That is, they come down to

eradicate falsehood and to establish truth in its stead. Or, in other words, it means, they come down to put into force the judgment of Allah.

[17 Al-Israa:89-93] "We have explained things for people in this Qur'an in diverse ways to make them understand the Message, yet most people obstinately persist in unbelief.

They said: "We shall not accept your Message until you cause a spring to gush forth for us from the earth; or that there be a garden of palms and vines for you and then you cause rivers to abundantly flow forth through them; or cause the sky to fall on us in pieces as you claimed, or bring Allah and the angels before us, face to face; or that there come to be for you a house of gold, or that you ascend to the sky - though we shall not believe in your ascension (to the sky) - until you bring down a book for us that we can read." Say to them, (O Muhammad): "Holy is my Lord! Am I anything else than a human being, who bears a Message (from Allah)?"

The eloquence of this concise answer is above praise. You demand from me that I should cause a spring to gush forth, or in the twinkling of an eye should bring into being a garden in full bloom with canals flowing in it, or I should cause the heaven to fall into pieces on those of you who are rejecting the message, or I should cause to build a furnished palace of gold, or I should call Allah and the angels to stand before you and testify to the effect that We Ourselves have sent down Muhammad as Our Messenger, or I should go up to the sky in your presence and bring down, addressed to you, the letter of authority of my appointment, duly signed by Allah so that you may touch it with your hands and read it with your own eyes. The concise answer to these big demands was this: My Lord be glorified! Have I ever claimed to be anything more than a human Messenger?

It may be expanded like this: O people, have I claimed to be God that you are demanding such things from me? Did I ever say that I am all powerful and am ruling over the earth and the Heavens? From the very first day my claim has been that I am a human being who is bringing the Message from Allah. Therefore, if you want to judge the authenticity of my claim, you may judge it from my message. If you are convinced that it is based on the truth and is absolutely rational, then you should believe in it without making foolish demands. On the other hand, if you find any defect in it, you may reject it. If you want to test whether my claim is based on truth, you should judge it by the standard of my conduct, and morals as a human being, and my mission. Is it not a folly that, instead of this, you are demanding from me to cleave the earth and cause the sky to fall? Is there any connection whatsoever of Prophethood with things like that?

[17 Al-Israa:94-95] Whenever Guidance came to people, nothing prevented them from believing except that they said: "Has Allah sent a human being as a Messenger?" Say: "Had angels been walking about in peace on the earth, We would surely have sent to them an angel from the heavens as Messenger."

This is to say that a Messenger does not merely convey the message, but is sent to reform human life in accordance with it. He has to apply the principles of the message to the circumstances of human beings, and has himself to practically demonstrate those principles. Moreover, he has to remove the misunderstandings of those people who try to listen to, and understand his message. Besides this, he has to organize and train the believers to create a society based on the teachings of his message.

He has to struggle against those who reject and oppose his message in order to subdue those powers that are bent upon corruption, and bring about the reformation for which Allah has sent His Messenger. As all these things have to be done in a society of human beings only a human Messenger can perform the mission. If an angel had been sent as a Messenger, the most he could have done was to convey the message, for he could not live among human beings and share their life and problems in order to reform them. It is thus clear that a human Messenger only could be suitable for this purpose.

In contrast to the miserable plight of the disbelievers on the Day of Resurrection, the Believers will be protected from the hardships of that Day; they will be treated with honor, and will have a blissful place for midday rest. According to a Tradition, the Holy Prophet (saws) said: "I declare, on oath by Allah, in Whose hand is my life, that the long, horrible Day of Resurrection will be made very short and light for a Believer, as short and light as the time taken in offering an obligatory Prayer." (Musnad Ahmad)

"On that Day all other kingdoms, which deluded man in the world, will come to an end, and there will be only the Kingdom of Allah. Who is the real Sovereign of the universe. In Chapter Mu'min: 16, the same thing has been stated thus: "On that Day when all the people will stand exposed, and nothing of them will be hidden from Allah, it will be asked, `Whose is the Sovereignty today?' The response from every side will be: Of Allah, the Almighty'." According to a Tradition, the Holy Prophet (saws) said, "Allah will take the heavens in one hand and the earth in the other, and will declare, I am the Sovereign. I am the Ruler. Where are the other rulers of the earth? Where are those tyrants? Where are the arrogant people?" (Musnad Ahmad, Bukhari, Muslim, and Abu Da'ud)

"Satan has proved very treacherous to man" may also be a part of the disbelievers lament, or it may be a remark by Allah, in which case the meaning will be: "And Satan is indeed the one who always deceives man."

The Arabic word mahjur is capable of several meanings. As such, the sentence may mean:" "these people did not regard the Qur'an as worthy of their consideration. They neither accepted it nor followed it"; or "They considered it to be nonsense, the delirium of insanity, or "They made it the target of their ridicule and mockery."

[25 Al-Furqaan:31] O Muhammad, in this very way We have made the criminals the enemies of every Prophet, but your Lord suffices for you as your Guide and Helper.

It is not a new thing that the disbelievers have become your enemies, for it has always been so with all the former Prophets and Messengers. See also (Chapter Al-Anaam, verses 112-113).

[6 Al-Anaam:112-113] "And so it is that against every Prophet We have set up the evil ones from among men and jinn. Some of them inspire others with false speech by way of delusion. Had it been your Lord's will, they would not have done it. Leave them alone to fabricate what they will. So that the hearts of those who do not believe in the Life to Come, might incline towards this attractive delusion, and may be well pleased with it, and might acquire the evils that they are bent on acquiring."

The Prophet (saws) is told that he should not be unnerved, even if the evil ones among both mankind, and jinn stood united against him, and opposed him with all their might. For this was not the first time that such a thing had happened. Whenever a Prophet came and tried to lead people to the Truth, all the satanic forces joined hands to defeat his mission. Deceptive talk signifies all the trickery, and maneuvering to which the enemy resorts. All his efforts are aimed at sowing doubts about Islam, and undermining people's faith in it, so as to arouse them against both the Prophet (saws), and his message. Taken as a whole, these are characterized as delusions. The weapons used in the crusade by the opponents of the Truth, have the effect of deluding others as well as themselves, no matter how beneficial and successful those weapons may appear to be.

Furthermore, we should always bear in mind that, according to the Qur'an, there is a tremendous difference between Allah's will and Allah's good pleasure. The failure to differentiate between the two, often gives rise to serious misconceptions. If a certain thing takes place in accord with the universal will of Allah, and by His sanction, does not necessarily mean that Allah is pleased with it. Nothing at all, takes place in the world, unless Allah permits it to take place. Unless He makes it a part of His scheme, and unless He makes it possible for that event to take place by creating its necessary conditions.

The act of stealing on the part of a thief, the act of homicide on the part of a murderer, the wrong and corruption of the wrong-doer and the corrupt, the unbelief of the unbeliever, and the polytheism of the polytheist, none of these are possible without the will of Allah. Likewise, the faith of the believer, and the piety of the pious are inconceivable without the will of Allah. In short, both these events require the will of Allah.

However, whereas the things in the first category do not please Him, those in the second do. Even though the will of Allah is oriented to ultimate good, the course of the realization of that good is paved with conflict between the forces of light and darkness, of good and evil, of what is sound and pure on the one hand, and what is corrupt and defiled on the other. With larger interests in view, Allah has endowed man with the disposition of obedience, as well as disobedience. He has created in man Abrahamic and Mosaic as well as Nimrodic and Pharaonic potentialities. Both the pure, unchanged human nature, and the satanic urges are ingrained in man's being, and have been provided with the opportunity to work themselves out, by coming into conflict with each other. He has granted those species of His creatures, who are have been endowed with authority (man and jinn) the freedom to choose between good and evil. Whosoever chooses to act righteously has been given the power to do so, and the same is the case with him who chooses to be evil.

People of both categories are in a position to use material resources within the framework of the broader considerations underlying Allah's governance of His universe. Allah will be pleased, however, only with those who are working for good. Allah likes His creatures to exercise their freedom of choice properly, and commit themselves to good, of their own volition. Unlike the angels, who carry out Allah's commands without resistance, the task entrusted to men is to strive to establish the way of life sanctioned by Allah in the face of opposition and hostility from evil-doers and rebels against Him. In the framework of His universal will, Allah allows even those who have chosen the path of rebellion to strive for the realization of their goals, even as He grants the believers every opportunity to strive along the path of obedience and service to Allah.

Despite this granting of freedom and choice to all, there is no doubt that Allah is pleased with, and guides, directs, supports and strengthens the believers alone, because their overall direction is to His liking. Nevertheless, they should not expect that by His supernatural intervention Allah will either force those who are disinclined to believe into believing, or that He will forcibly remove the satanic forces among both men and jinn, who are resolved to spare neither their mental and physical energy, nor their material resources to impede the triumph of the Truth.

Those determined to strive in the cause of the Truth, virtue and righteousness are told that they must prove their earnest devotion by waging a fierce struggle against the devotees of falsehood. For had Allah wanted to use miracles to obliterate falsehood, and usher in the reign of the Truth, He would not have required human beings to accomplish the task. He could have simply seen to it that no evil one remained in the world, leaving no possibility for polytheism and unbelief to exist.

It is Our Law that the criminals will always oppose the truth. You should, therefore, pursue your mission with full confidence, and determination without expecting immediate results. Guidance does not only imply bestowing knowledge of the truth, but it also means giving the right guidance, at the right time to guide the Islamic movement on the right lines, and to defeat the strategy and scheme of the enemies of Islam. Help means all kinds of moral, spiritual and material help to the followers of the truth in their conflict against falsehood. Thus, Allah is All Sufficient for the righteous people and they need no other support, provided they have full faith in Allah, and fight falsehood with all their energies and strength.

This means to encourage the Prophet (saws), otherwise the previous assertion would have been very discouraging without this. It means to say: Even if the unbelievers have become your enemies, you should continue your mission, for We shall guide you in every stage and situation, and help you against them. We shall defeat all the schemes of your enemies and help you in every way in your conflict with falsehood. We shall provide you with material means also, but you should trust in Us and exert your utmost against falsehood.

Lightning Source UK Ltd.
Milton Keynes UK
UKHW010906290920
370727UK00001B/49